GM Muscle Cars

Bill Holder and Phil Kunz

MBI Publishing Company

FFirst published in 2002 by MBI Publishing Company, Galtier Plaza, Suite 200, 380 Jackson Street, St. Paul, MN 55101-3885 USA

MBI Publishing Company books are also available at discounts in bulk quantity for industrial or sales-promotional use. For details write to Special Sales Manager at Motorbooks International Wholesalers & Distributors, Galtier Plaza, Suite 200, 380 Jackson Street, St. Paul, MN 55101-3885 USA.

Library of Congress Cataloging-in-Publication Data Available

ISBN 0-7603-1175-7

Edited by Amy Glaser

On the front cover:
A 1969 Pontiac GTO Judge. *Mike Mueller*

On the frontispiece:
Two versions of the powerful 454-ci engine were available for the 1970 Chevelle SS. The LS-5 360 horsepower and the LS-6 450 horsepower versions surpassed the power levels of the 396, but their stay at those monster levels lasted far too short a time period.

On the title page:
Because the looks of the 1966 GTO were so successful, few changes were made in the 1967 GTO's appearance. The parking lights were still located in the grille openings, but the texture of the grille was of a wider pattern.

On the acknowledgments page:
The body styling for the 1960 Vette stayed pretty much the same as in previous years. The side body scallops were very popular, shown here in silver. Also, note the wide whitewall tires on this startling beauty.

On the back cover:
The 1969 Hurst Olds was one of the sharpest muscle cars ever produced. Garbed in Cameo White and Firefrost Gold, this machine carries a H/O 455 engine capable of 380 horsepower. This car is owned by Robert Lamons. The awesome Gran Sport was Buick's successful attempt at a muscle car. This cold-black example is owned by Steve Wegh. The 1971 model is powered by a 350-ci, 260 horsepower engine.

Printed in China

Contents

Acknowledgments

The authors wish to thank the following car owners for allowing their cars to be photographed for this book: Steve Wegh, Dave Clemmons, James Stamper, Greg Stout, Doug Alsip, John Kocara, John Duncan, Bob Lamons, Tony Burk, Bob Cline, and Mark Stevens.

Introduction

It was a shining-star time period from a performance point of view, an era that will live forever in automotive history. The mid-1960s through the early 1970s brought forth performance and styling that had never been seen before. It was as if the factories were turning out purebred racecars and selling them from dealership showrooms. These cars were called "Muscle Cars."

The amazing aspect of this phenomena was the fact that the Big Three, and even American Motors, were all competing to sell these high-powered products. The horsepower, for the most part, was generated by big cubic inches, big compression ratios, and big carburetors or, in some cases, multiple carbs. The power figures quoted for the big-block powerplants of the era were startling, in a number of cases exceeding 400 horsepower. Add a light body plus suitable suspension, and breathless performance was inevitable.

Almost all of the divisions in the large companies were involved with this chase, including the Plymouth and Dodge divisions of Chrysler; the Ford and Mercury divisions of Ford; and the Buick, Chevrolet, Oldsmobile, and Pontiac divisions of General Motors (GM). Each division had its unique performance engines, and each model and brand had its own cult of devoted buying fans.

Buick was possibly the most surprising GM division to delve into the muscle phenomena. Normally associated with prestige models, Buick didn't have a performance image, but that certainly changed during this period. Buick's Gran Sport, Stage 1, and GSX models were as quick, or quicker, than most of the competition. The division's top

Buick surprised everyone when it decided to build muscle cars. This '70 GS Stage 1 was one of the top Buick performance machines.

powerplant was a 455-ci Stage 1 mill capable of 360 announced horsepower. In reality, the engine produced much more!

Then came the Chevy line, which included five models with muscle connotations: Chevelle, Nova, Corvette, Camaro, and Monte Carlo.

The Vette in the 1950s used muscular versions of the 327-ci engine. In the 1960s, both the Vette and Camaro were first fitted with powerful 350-ci engines before moving to big-block powerplants. The top Vette engine would be the awesome 427, while the Camaro's largest powerplant would be a 396-ci engine, although certain special models also carried a 427-ci mill. The largest engine for the Nova would be a 402. The Chevelle was fitted with

The Chevy division offered muscular engines in its Chevelle, Nova, Corvette, Camaro, and Monte Carlo models. This 417 COPO Camaro was a low-production model rated at 425 horsepower.

both the potent 396-ci and 454-ci engines. A 454 was also the biggest engine for the Monte Carlo.

Oldsmobile accomplished similar success with its performance 442 model, which could be purchased with a number of bullish powerplants. The 442 was fitted with a number of different engines, up to a 455 with 365 horsepower.

There were a number of performance "W" modifications to the Olds muscle cars, including the W-30, W-31, and W-32 versions, with featured upgraded looks and powerplant performance tweaks. The top engine was the W-30 with 370 horses. Also, there were the Hurst Olds models that emphasized an external performance look, and the engines under their hoods matched that impression.

Pontiac had long been associated with motorsports and high performance, so its entry into the muscle-car fray was easy and expected. Its performance image was established earlier with the

For Pontiac, the GTO epitomized performance and power. The first version came in 1964 and featured a triple-carbed 389-ci powerplant. This particular GTO is a 1968 version, with a 400-ci powerplant under the hood. Pontiac also offered muscle Firebirds and Trans Ams with outstanding performance capabilities.

heavy Grand Prix models of the early 1960s. With multi-carbed 428 powerplants, the Grand Prix models were killer machines!

But for most, the Pontiac muscle-car image was initiated with the GTO family, first introduced in 1964 with the vaunted triple-carb powerplant. The engine size would continue to grow to 455 cubic inches during its heyday. There was also a flashy version of the GTO called "The Judge" that attracted a ton of attention. The Judge had the same engine as the GTO, but this version was a looker!

In 1967, Pontiac added another star to its muscle-car galaxy with the potent Firebird/Trans Am family. A sporty model with genes that tied it to the Chevy Camaro, the model introduced big-time power to the sports-car set. Performance was definitely the name of the game with a family of Ram-Air 400-cubic-inch engines, followed by even more powerful 455-ci engines.

The most powerful version of the 455-ci engine was the so-called 455 Super Duty that was out-and-out a pure racing engine. The Super Duty remains one of the most desired collectable muscle engines to this day.

What a performance era it was, and GM was right at the forefront.

Several Oldsmobile muscle cars of the late 1960s and early 1970s featured legendary performance capabilities, including the 442, the W-30/31/32 series, and the Hurst models. Shown is a '70 442 W-30.

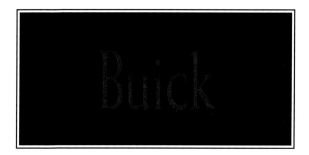

Chapter 1

Considered straight-laced and conservative, Buick cars were normally thought of as heavy four-door monsters. In the mid-1960s, it was an image that Buick was trying to shake. A Buick may very well be the family car that you grew up with. A Buick represented solidarity, and in the minds of some, it was an indication of a person's success in business. Buick projected all those images, but one image it still didn't have was that of a muscle car. No way! All that would soon change with the advent of the Gran Sport and the follow-up Stage 1 and GSX models. It was an amazing transformation.

This '71 Gran Sport shows its style from this front view. Note the horizontal stripes over the blacked-out grille and the red-lettered GS on the left side. The macho five-spoke wheels also gave the GS a look of high performance, opposed to the luxury look that Buick had been associated with for so long.

The Gran Sport (GS)

With the GS model, which was introduced in 1965 and lasted through the 1972 model year, Buick created an authentic muscle car and developed its unique muscle reputation. Not unlike many other GM muscle models of the period, the GS began life as an option of another model, the established Skylark. The GS option came along mid-1965 and included both performance and appearance aspects.

Included in the package was, most importantly, a brutish 401-ci powerplant rated at 325 horsepower at 4400 rpm. Actually, the corporate rule at the time was that there wasn't to be any displacement above 400, but somehow the GS's 401 slipped through. In addition to its impressive power, the 401 put out 445 pounds-feet of torque. A Carter AFB provided the fuel management with the compression ratio at 10:1, which was high for the time period. For the real performance-oriented, there was even a dealer-installed dual four-barrel carburetor option. On the GS models, the stock Skylark body was given a performance edge with red GS emblems on the roof quarters, deck, and grille.

A number of flashy appearance options on the '66 GS made it look a lot more like a muscle car. The hood ornament was deleted, but fake air scoops, a blacked-out grille, and side striping were added. The GS was maturing fast, but it was still not a model on its own.

The 1966 GS was fitted with basically the same 401 engine, which was officially known as the Wildcat 455. There's an interesting story on the nomenclature of the engine and the reason why there was a discrepancy of 54 between the two numbers. Normally, companies at the time liked to flaunt the number of cubic inches in the naming of their engines; in the case of the 401 engine, its torque rating (increased 10 to 455

pounds-feet for 1966) was more impressive than its displacement, so the engine was named Wildcat 455, rather than Wildcat 401.

For 1967, two versions of the GS were offered. The NR-coded 401 engine remained, although the horsepower rating was given a 15-horse boost to 340 and the model was dubbed "Skylark GS400." The GS400 featured a pair of hood scoops, a new grille design, and striping. The GS nametag was also tagged to a lower-powered version, the GS340, which carried a 340-ci, 260-horsepower (NR-coded) powerplant. It was a pretty impressive performance from a small block! Significant changes were made to the 400 engine, including larger intake and exhaust valves for better flow. Exhaust flow was further increased by the 400's larger manifolds. To effectively apply those horses to the ground, several rear-end gear ratios were offered. With manual transmissions, a 3.55:1 rear end was available unless air conditioning was also ordered. On special order, 3.90:1 or 4.30:1 positraction gears were also available. This was definitely not the Buick of the past!

As a low-production option, the GS340 was available in only two colors: silver or white. The GS340 was obviously aimed at those who weren't quite ready to pay for big-block performance. This more-streetable model received significant raves. Unfortunately, it was discontinued at the end of the model year.

It's interesting that the corporate advertising for the 1967 GS included all the expected Buick words such as big, roomy, and comfortable, however, it also included another surprising word that was most applicable: muscular.

For the 1968 model year, the GS became a model on its own and used the brand-new B Body as its base. All the 1968 GS models took on performance looks for this model year with simulated

For 1969, the GS was offered with a pair of punchy mills: A 400-ci engine producing 340 horsepower at 5000 rpm and the 350-ci engine shown here, which was capable of 280 horses. Even though the 350 had fewer cubes, it was still capable of impressive performance.

air scoops on the fenders and a lower-body accent stripe. On the GS400, the classy-looking hood scoops were functional. Increased spring rates improved handling.

For 1968, the small-block GS model was the GS350, named for its new 350-ci, 280-horsepower engine. The GS400 was also back, in hardtop and convertible versions. The 350's extra power was a result of its larger intake and exhaust manifolds from the 430-ci powerplant (the change was made for emission reasons), rather than the 10 ci of added displacement. The new 350 worked so well, it was carried over through the next two years of GS production. The most popular GS was the GS400 hardtop, with 10,743 sold. Next was the GS350, with 8,317 sold. GS400 convertibles were the rarest of the breed, as they still are today, with only 2,454 sold.

Induction was a new key word for the 1969 model year. The twin hood-mounted scoops on the GS400 fed cool air to the engine through a special twin-snorkel air cleaner. Although an official power increase was not announced, the scoops increased engine appreciability.

The RR-coded 400-ci engine carried a 340 horsepower rating, made at 5,000 rpm, while the RP-coded 350-ci engine could provide an impressive 280 horses. There was also a change in the carburetor, the former Carter AFB was deleted in favor of a 750-cfm Rochester four-barrel. Powered

Buick officially called it the Gran Sport, but it wouldn't be long before the catchy GS name would be attached to the Buick muscle machine. The GS was first offered as an option, but later it would be a separate model.

The design of the '69 GS was sweeping and stylish. A body crease stretched from the top of the front quarter and curved down to the front of the rear wheel opening. Front-end details included twin headlights and a horizontal bar across the middle of the grille meshing.

by the 400-ci engine, the 1969 GS was capable of quarter-mile times in the mid-14-second range. The muscle era was nearing its peak, and the GS was a big player in the game.

It was the cylinder head design that really generated the power for the GS400 engine. Compared with the so-called "Nail-Head" design used on earlier GS engines, these heads carried larger 2-inch-diameter intakes and 1.625-inch-diameter exhausts. The flow characteristics of the powerplant were also increased by the partial wedge design of the combustion chamber.

The '69 GS body style showed a slight revision from the previous year, with a curving body stripe reaching from the front quarter to the rear-wheel cutout and the "GS" as well as the "350" or "400" numeral markings were highly visible. The grille featured a single horizontal bar and vertical bars. Unfortunately, the performance and cosmetic changes were not enough to provide a large increase in buyers.

In 1970, things just couldn't have become any better. Performance was still the name of the game with the 350-ci engine edging up to a 315-horse rating, not far from the 1 horsepower-per-cubic-inch goal. The punchy mill acquired the rating at 4800 rpm, but was just as impressive from the torque point of view, with a 410-pounds-feet rating. As impressive as the 350-ci engine continued to be, it was lost in the hoopla of the introduction of a new 455-ci big block for the GS455. Yet, the 455 didn't provide a big performance increase; its rating of 350 horsepower was just 10 horsepower more than that of the previous 400 engine. The big difference in the two powerplants came in the torque department, where the 455 excelled at 510 pounds-feet, possibly the highest ever in the muscle era, and made it at only 2800 rpm.

As high as the 455's horsepower rating was, it was thought at the time to be lower than the engine's actual power output. For example, how could basically the same powerplant be quoted at 370

15

The '70 GS's macho looks bespoke the performance that it carried under the hood. The twin scoops on the hood were functional and funneled cool air directly into the carburetor's air cleaner. Shown is a 1970 GS convertible.

horses in the Riviera application? It came right down to the fact that insurance rates skyrocketed with horsepower increases on these Buick muscle versions. The increased displacement of the 455 was made by enlarging the bore from 4.040 to 4.315 inches, while the stroke remained unchanged at 3.90 inches. The 455 components were "full race," with wedge-shaped combustion chambers, aluminum pistons, forged rods, and a nodular iron crank. Topside, a 730-cfm Rochester four-barrel

carburetor performed the fuel management functions, aided greatly by functional hood air scoops.

The weight of the GS455 was still a beefy 3,800 pounds, but with that 455 boiling under the hood, the performance was still awe-inspiring: 14-second/98-mph quarter-mile capabilities. Zero-to-60 could be accomplished in just over 6 seconds.

The 1970 model year also saw a new look for Buick performance models to accompany the new power. The GS455 was fitted with a GS455

emblem on the blacked-out grille. The model is considered by many to be one of Buick's top muscle models. Additionally, those hood scoops really gave it a muscle look.

For 1971, the 455 engine was back, but things just weren't the same. The cubic-inch displacement was still in place, but the horsepower took a dive to only 315. The compression ratio was reduced by 15 percent, which was the main reason for the power reduction. The 350 engine was also back for 1970, but it wasn't exactly the same. The engine's horsepower rating was lowered to 260 horsepower,

a drop of 20 horses. Granted, the performance was down a bit, but make no mistake, these machines were still able performers on both street and strip.

The GS350 nomenclature was dropped for 1970, so the 350-powered cars carried only the GS nametag, while the GS455 name remained intact. The GS455 emblems were also still in place, although Buick didn't officially use the nomenclature in its advertising.

Production totals for the '71 GS were almost identical to those of the previous year: 8,268 hard-tops and 902 convertibles. Fortunately, even though the power was downgraded, the racy looks topside were retained. Included were bright rocker-panel moldings, blacked-out grille, still-functional hood scoops, and flashy trim. In 1972, the bottom dropped out for the GS, and performance was further reduced for the model, just as it was throughout the rest of the industry.

The Stage 1

The earlier GS models had performance, however, many buyers wanted more muscle unleashed when their right foot was stomped down. Fortunately, GM's former pure-luxury division was up to fulfilling that desire. Enter the so-called Stage 1 option. This pure-performance option kicked up the GS's already-potent performance so that it equaled or exceeded just about everything else on street or strip.

Even though the Stage 1 option was exactly that—an option—the name almost instantly stood on its own. You either had a Stage 1 car, or you didn't. As the years have passed, the attractiveness of these cars has only increased. The higher value of the Stage 1 has even caused a small number of GS owners to do a little innovative conversion work on their standard GSs, turning them into bogus Stage 1 machines.

It was a GS, but when this 1970 model carried this unique identification, it was a different beast. The "Stage 1" told Buick enthusiasts that this was one of the few with the killer 455 Stage 1 engine.

When you found a 1970 GS with the Stage 1 identification, you knew that you really had something. But if you are thinking about making the purchase of such a machine for restoration, make sure that you are getting the real thing because there are lots of phonies out there!

This beautiful 1970 Stage 1 carries the optional rear-deck spoiler, which was extremely effective at high speeds.

The Stage 1 modification was first offered on the 1968 GS400, as a dealer-installed option called the "Stage 1 Special Package," for race applications. The Stage 1 upgrades for this model year included a hotter cam, higher compression ratio, larger tail pipes, streamlined manifold, larger carburetor, and a positraction rear end. The joke about the powerplant was that it was rated at only 5 horsepower over the stock 400 engine. Reportedly, it was also possible to acquire parts later included in the '69 Stage 1 package as dealer-installed components on the 1968 GSs.

For 1969, the Stage 1 was a factory option, obtainable by checking off the option on the order sheet. For the $199.05 price, a buyer received an unbelievable combination of performance goodies,

There was no mistaking the distinctive induction system for the 1970 Stage 1 engine. The engine type was vividly announced by the Stage 1 name on the cleaner head itself.

a list of items that looked like it came from the local speed shop. The fact that a GS was a Stage car was noted under the hood with decals on the valve covers and air cleaner. The optional list of performance goodies included a custom high-lift camshaft, fast-flow fuel pump, a specially-calibrated Quadrajet carburetor on a cast-iron intake, and a high-pressure lubrication system. Exhaust was free flowing with a massive, 2.5-inch dual exhaust. The twin scoops on the hood were functional and pushed cool air directly into that big carburetor. A special linkage was designed to open the secondaries more quickly. The power was well applied to the pavement with a positraction rear end hooked with a 3.64:1 gearing.

The factory data indicated that the Stage 1 for 1969 had a rating of 350 horsepower at 5,000 rpm, a surprisingly minimal increase of only 10 horsepower over the stock GS400 engine. The torque for the Stage 1 engine was rated at an awesome 440 pounds-feet at 3,200 rpm. Performance Buicks were always noted for their punch at low speeds, and that was certainly the character of this machine. With the corporate battle for performance at the time, it's really surprising that more Stage 1s weren't built. With sales of only 1,256 cars, the 1969 Stage 1 was, and is, one of the most rare and desirable Buick muscle cars.

But in 1970, a new most-desired model was introduced: the GS455 Stage 1. This powerplant was definitely the big kahuna. Among the upgrades included in the Stage 1 package were dual valve springs, bigger valves, a hotter cam, high-pressure oil-pump relief spring, and richer carburetor settings.

Its performance put this Stage 1 at the top of the big-gun muscle cars of the era, actually being able to dip into the 13 second range at speeds in the 100-mph category, according to the car magazine tests. With its 360-horsepower rating, this car wasn't an example of fuel economy, which averaged in the 12—13 miles per gallon range, depending how hard the driver put down his foot. These Stage 1s come rare, and they definitely are expensive in today's collector market. Only 3,097 '70 Stage 1s were produced, and just 232 of them were the most desirable convertible models. The Stage 1 identification was now external, with "Stage 1" lettering right under the GS455 on the front fenders.

Nobody escaped the performance downgrades that started with the 1971 models, not even the Stage 1. Although the Stage 1 option would still be offered for several more years, like everything else during the power downturn, the Stage 1 went down with it.

The GSX

Just when the 1970 GS455 Stage 1 seemed like the ultimate, along came the snazzy GSX model that same year. Quite frankly, it was an externally dolled-up Stage 1.

This first GSX looked like a combination of a rocket and a racecar, with its snazzy body-length stripe that sported a kickup on the rear quarter. Broad stripes also swept down the scoop-infested hood with GSX decals in three external locations. In order to make this unique Buick really stand out, the 1970 version was offered in only two colors: Apollo White and Saturn Yellow. The majority of the initial GSXs were sprayed in the latter color. The GSX also featured an aft spoiler, a one-piece fiberglass unit that was bolted directly to the rear deck. In addition, there was also a fiberglass lower front spoiler, which was painted black.

Of course, that awesome 455 Stage 1 engine could be ordered with the GSX, but if that was too much power, a GSX with a more docile 455 engine was available.

There was no mistake of the identity of this distinctive inductive system for the 1970 Stage 1 engine.

A design highlight of the 1971 GSX was its body-length stripe that terminated by sweeping upward onto the spoiler. This graphic treatment gave the spoiler a look of being totally integrated with the body.

The 1970 GSX had rolled out with little fanfare in national advertising. As a result, many potential buyers just didn't seem to know of its existence, so many of the 1970 GSXs were still sitting on showroom floors when the 1971s started to arrive. A total of 698 1970 GSX models were built. Well over half (479) were built with the Stage 1 option, with 280 of that number also

getting the four-speed transmission. Reportedly, these particular GSXs were capable of 13-second quarter-mile performance.

The GSX was reduced to an option in its second and final year, 1971. Production was very minimal, a total of 124 vehicles. In order to acquire a GSX from the order sheet, the buyer had to check off the Special Car Order (SCO).

Notice that the GS was still a part of the GSX model, but the GS was printed in smaller letters. There was no doubt that the company wanted the GSX to be a flashy performance model on its own. It certainly succeeded.

Chapter 2

Within the Chevrolet Division a large number of muscle models evolved during the muscle car era, and the same muscle powerplants were used in a number of them. Chevy's muscle models included Chevelle, El Camino, Nova, Corvette, Camaro, and Monte Carlo.

Chevelle

The trend toward ever-increasing horsepower started at Chevrolet in the early 1960s with the 409 powerplant. To remain in the game, the division realized it would have to punch up the performance of its mid-sized model line.

Chevy looked to Chevelle in 1964, with its macho Super Super (SS) model, as being a good place to start. Options such as a tachometer, sport

Check out the macho look of this 1966 Chevelle SS convertible. This cold, black machine carries the matching blacked-out grille with the centered SS letters. Note the sweeping look of the side sheet metal.

steering wheel, chrome trim items, and gauges gave the SS its sporting image. It was a great-looking machine, but there still wasn't that much power under the hood. Its 283-ci engine was good for only 195 horsepower. Even the mid-year introduction of a 327-ci engine didn't solve the horsepower image problem that the Chevelle was facing. The 327 was rated at a respectable 300 horses (a 250-horse version was also available), but the 327s were still a far cry from the big blocks that were now in the showrooms of the enemy camps.

That all changed in 1965. The magic numbers were suddenly 396 and 375, cubic inches and horsepower, respectively. Characteristics of the magnificent new engine included a forged crank, cast-iron heads, and an 800-cfm Holley carb, all decked out in a neatly detailed engine compartment.

The new heavy-hauler Chevelle was called the Z-16, and a number of significant modifications were made to be the Z-16 chassis. First, in order to accept the increased power and torque of the new engine, the frame was beefed up and a stronger suspension with new stabilizer bars was fitted. Other modifications included full-size 11-inch brakes, quicker steering, and special heavy-duty shocks and springs. Only 201 Z-16s were built.

The 396-powered Chevelle for 1966 (now called the "SS396") was a more streetable vehicle than the Z-16 had been. The standard 396 was now rated at 325 horses (50 horsepower less that the Z-16 396), but the optional L34 version was rated at 360 horsepower, courtesy of its special

The Z-16 was the first Chevelle to answer the muscle-car call. Its 396 engine was rated at 375 horses. Only 201 Z-16s were built, and few have been located. Here's one of the best, the 1990 restoration owned by Harold Vieth of Iowa.

cam. Near the end of the year, the 375-horsepower L78 was offered. The 1966 SS396 featured simulated hood intakes, vinyl interiors, "Super Sport" script lettering on the rear quarter, and "SS396" emblems. A great year for Chevy, the SS396 model sold an impressive 72,272 units in both convertible and hardtop styles.

In 1967, the standard 325- and optional L78 375-horse ratings remained unchanged. The optional L34's rating was reduced to 350 horsepower. Appearance-wise, the SS396 featured a blacked-out grille, "SS396" emblems, and other appearance options. Chevy built 63,006 SS396s for the year. The Chevelle SS was completely new for 1968. New appearance features included extensions on the lower body moldings, taillight panels, and a completely redesigned dash. The 325-horse powerplant was again the standard powerplant for the SS396 in 1968. The optional 340-horse L34 and 375-horse L78 versions were listed as options.

Slight appearance changes were made to the '69 SS. The big-block engine offerings were basically unchanged, but a new small-block option was introduced: the 300-horsepower L48 350-ci engine.

The most powerful of the Chevelles was not a completely factory-built machine. The so-called Yenko Chevelles were a special breed of the model that were modified by the Yenko Chevy dealership in Cannonsburg, Pennsylvania. Only 99 of the machines were built for 1969; about 35 of them are known to still exist.

The look of the '67 Chevelle SS was little different from the previous year's model. Its front-end design was slightly changed, with a new horizontal bar grille. The 396 engine was a big selling point for the SS this model year.

The awesome 427-ci powerplant was first offered in the Chevelle for 1969. It was carried by both the COPO and Yenko (shown here) machines. With 425 horses, the powerplant would be under a Chevelle hood for only one year.

This '69 big block was the kingpin of the 396-ci engines. Three versions were available, with ratings of 325, 350, and 375 horses. The 375-horse engine is shown. From a twenty-first century collector's point of view, this is the engine you want, and you'll pay a large sum of money to get it.

The Yenkos were power personified with the awesome 425-horsepower L72 427-ci powerplant squeezed under the hood. There were also a number of additional appearance items added to the Yenko Chevelles, including special Yenko striping, Rally wheels, and extra gauges. In addition, there were a very few special Chevrolet Office Production Order (COPO) Chevelles built, all in 1969. These cars carried the same 427-ci engines as the Yenkos, and only a very few of these have been located; needless to say, these cars are very desirable to collectors.

Many Chevy performance fans consider the 1970 Chevelle the best and most desirable of the division's muscle machines. That opinion relates directly back to the introduction of the bone-jarring 450-horsepower LS-6 454-ci powerplant. The new engine came as a part of the SS454 option, and listed for a minimal $263.

The LS-6 used 11.25:1 compression heads, a special solid-lifter cam, aluminum intake, forged crank, and a giant 780-cfm Holley carb. A slightly lesser model of the 454 was the LS-5 version, capable of a reported 360 horsepower. Two potent 396 engines were available: the 350-horse L34 and the 375-horse L78. These 396 engines from 1970 and on actually had a displacement of 402 ci, but because of the aura of the 396 numbers, they remained in place.

Even as pressure mounted in 1971 to stop the production of big-block engines, the SS454s remained popular. Two 454 engines were once again available. For 1971, the LS-6 was rated at 425 horsepower and the LS-5 was rated at 365. Even though the sweet lines of the Chevelle body style were still in place for 1972, its performance was greatly decreased. The LS-6's rating was lowered by 25 horses. The LS-3 396-ci engine was also available, but it was a weak imitation of its earlier smokin' brothers.

The flowing lines of the '70 Chevelle SS are clearly seen from this view. The body sides were completely devoid of chrome, with the exception of the SS letters on the front quarters.

El Camino

The El Camino truck conversion used Chevelle sheet metal and powerplants during the performance era. As such, it was possible to acquire a majority of the same high-performance engines of the Chevelle.

Model year 1970 was also the first year for the powerful 454-ci powerplant in the El Camino. Although the engine was publicized with the '70 Chevelle, it certainly deserves a second look in this car/truck application

The unique Cowl Induction hood was a significant attention-grabber on the 1969 El Camino SS. The classy truck was basically a Chevelle, except for the rear end.

Probably the most desirable of all the performance Novas was the Yenko version for the 1966 model year. It was called the Yenko Deuce and featured classy detailing, including a body-length stripe.

Nova

The sedate, domestic, and economical image that the Nova model carried during the early 1960s certainly made it an odd candidate for transformation into a performance model. However, during the last half of the 1960s, Chevy transformed this domestic model into a performance vehicle. By 1966, the Nova was available with the potent L30 275-horsepower version of the tried-and-true 327 powerplant. The real killer was the single-year L79 version of that same engine, which was capable of an impressive 350 horses. The L79's power, combined with the Nova's ton-and-one-half gross weight, made the model a real street performer.

The mainstay engine for the 1967 Nova was the L30 327-ci mill, which picked up 5 horsepower to total 280. The Nova SS body had been revised to give it the aura of a performance car.

For 1968, the L48 350-ci engine with a rated 295 horsepower was the standard powerplant. The SS350 package featured simulated scoops on the hood and a blacked-out grille and rear-deck panel, along with front- and rear-mounted SS tags. To increase that ever-important performance image for 1968, Chevy also equipped a limited number of Nova SSs with the awesome L78 375-horse 396. Even more exclusive was the optional L89 396, which was also rated at 375 horsepower, but was equipped with aluminum heads. The slightly less awesome 350-horse L34 396 was also available on the 1968 Nova SS. Just 667 Novas that year were equipped with the L78, 234 with the L34, and with the L89.

The L48 350 engine was rated at 300 horsepower for 1969, in a year where there were a minimal number of changes in the outward appearance of the SS. Quietly, though, it was still possible to acquire specially prepared Nova SSs that carried all three versions of the 396.

But as was true with the Chevelle and Camaro, Yenko modifications would also play here too, with the Yenko SYC 427 Nova. The engines were not factory-installed, but (like the Chevelle) squeezed into position by the aforementioned Yenko Chevrolet dealership. They were few in number, only 30 to be exact. The cars arrived at the dealership carrying the L78 396 engines, which were replaced by the L72 427-ci, 425-horsepower powerhouses. There were also reportedly a very few factory 427 Novas constructed. Only about a half dozen of these machines have been located, and their rarity makes them—along with the Yenko Novas—the most valuable of the Nova muscle models.

For 1970, the standard engine for the Nova was a 300-horse version of the 350 engine, but the Nova could still be ordered with a big block. Although the L34 and L78 396 engines weren't advertised in the showroom literature, they could still be had on special order. There was yet another Nova for both 1969 and 1970, but it wasn't listed in any sales literature. It was called the Yenko

Deuce and carried the LT-1 Corvette version of the 350 engine, which knocked out 370 willing ponies. Other powertrain components included the Turbo 400 transmission controlled by a Hurst shifter and a 12-bolt 4.11:1 rear end. These models, of course, carried the distinctive Yenko body detailing.

Model year 1971 was the beginning of the end for high-power Novas, because the big blocks were discontinued and the remaining small blocks lost horsepower, as Chevy lowered compression ratios in most of its engines. The new Rally Nova model featured a 245-horsepower version of the 350, while the SS version of the 350 was rated at only 260 horses on regular gas.

On the contrary, some data indicates that certain 1971 Novas were equipped with 454 engines. At that time, the 454s were available in Monte Carlos and Chevelles, but anything was possible.

Corvette

Many enthusiasts consider the Corvette a sports car versus a muscle car, a connotation that originated during the 1950s when the car was

The muscle era began in the 1950s for the Corvette, as proved by this twin-carbed 283-ci engine. This 1957 engine came in 245- and 270-horsepower versions. With a car weight of just over 2,700 pounds, this combination made for a real muscle machine.

Not only did the Vette have big horses under the hood, it also had great looks on the outside. The design featured a front end carrying twin headlights, a vertical bar grille, and a sculpted hood.

introduced with relatively small-displacement powerplants. That all changed in the 1960s when the model was fitted with some of the industry's largest and most powerful engines, making it one of the top performers in the growing list of evolving muscle cars.

The Corvette's 283-ci engine was capable of exactly 283 horsepower, some heavy performance for a machine weighing in at only 2,730 pounds. Dual-carb versions of the 283 powerplants were rated at 245 and 270 horsepower in 1958. A fuel-

injected version made 290 horses. So it was made clear that even though displacement was low, the muscle era for the Vette really started in the 1950s.

By 1960, the fuel-injected 283 was rated at an impressive 315 horsepower. That high-performance option cost a healthy (for the time period) $484. The dual-carbed 283 horsepower rating peaked out at 275 horses in 1961.

Model year 1962 was significant for the Corvette because of the introduction of the 327-ci powerplant. The top fuel-injected version was

Fuel injection was a popular option for late 1950s Corvette powerplants. The two versions of the 1959 283-injected Vette mill were capable of 250- and 290-horsepower ratings.

rated at 360 horses. A pair of dual-carb versions were rated at 300 and 340 horsepower. The use of the familiar "L" engine designations began in 1963 with the L75 300-horsepower 327-ci, the L76 340-horsepower 327-ci, and the L84 360-horsepower 327-ci engines. Then, in 1964, the L84 power was increased by an additional 15 horsepower.

The end of the L84 came in the mid-1960s with the killer L78 396-ci powerplant. Although the 396 powerplants would prove popular in other Chevy models for several years, the L78 was only a one-year deal with Vette.

But this was the mid-1960s time period, and manufacturers couldn't sit still during the horsepower wars. The '66 Vette model year saw the

introduction on two monstrous 427-ci powerplants. The L72 version was rated conservatively at 425 horses, while the tamer L36 model was advertised at 390 horses. A special "Power Bulge" hood came with the 427-equipped Vettes. The L72 powerplant had significantly more performance than the 396 L78, kicking the torque up from the L78's 415 to an unbelievable 460 pounds-feet. The L72 engine, which completely filled the Vette's engine compartment, featured solid lifters and was capable, according to *Car and Driver* magazine, of being a 12-second,112-miles per hour performer on the drag strip. The standard L72 transmission was a four-speed.

But there was also significant small-block power for 1966: the 300-horsepower 327-ci

The 1962 Vette's front end had a macho look, with a blacked-out hood and other front openings. The headlight rims were done in body color, giving the model more of a street-machine look. Although many loved this body style, 1962 would be its final hurrah.

powerplant. Available with both three- and four-speed manual transmissions, a '66 Vette equipped with this engine proved to be a real sleeper performance model. Then came 1967, and the capable 427 had been kicked up a few notches with both 430- and 435-horse versions available, followed by the L68 400-horse model. With three carbs, solid lifters, and high-compression heads, the 435-horse L71 engine ($437 extra) was something else! In fact, many stated that the factory's horsepower rating was greatly understated. The L71 was the only Vette engine to ever use three carbs, and it was

available from 1967 to 1969. If that wasn't enough, there was an aluminum head option for an additional $389. When equipped with that modification, the combination became known as the L89 and was rated at an identical 435 horses.

Finally, for 1967, there was the awesome L88 version, and there's an interesting story about this Vette model. It was a limited production model, and only 20 were produced its first year. Outwardly, the L88 didn't appear any different from any other 427 Vette, but fire it up, and you quickly learned this was a different beast. It wasn't built for the populace, but to race, and it was a tiger in Sports Car Club of America (SCCA) competition.

The engine featured an unheard-of 12.5:1 compression ratio, aluminum heads, four-bolt mains, aluminum pistons, forged rods, and a monstrous Holley 850-cfm carb sitting topside. Dragstrip performance for this machine was what you might expect, with elapsed times in the quarter mile close to the 11-second category at about 115 mph. Even though the L88 was never advertised for public consumption, there were still a limited number that were purchased. One hundred and sixteen of the L88-equipped Corvette coupes were sold in 1969, its final year.

High-horsepower powerplants were back for 1968, along with a brand-new body design for the Vette. All the same 427 powerplants were available,

but it would be the final year for the powerful engine. The top horsepower 327 in 1968 was the L79 version, capable of 350 horses, an option costing $105.

The big change for 1969 was the introduction of the new 350-horsepower 350-ci engine, designated the LT-1. Performance add-ons included aluminum intake manifolds, high-compression heads, and an 800-cfm Holley four-barrel carb. For 1970, the power ratings of the LT-1 were kicked up 20 to 370 horses, some very heavy performance numbers for a small block. It wasn't cheap either, costing an additional $447 for the option. After 1970, the LT-1's horsepower rating started a steep decline. For 1971, it was back down to 350 and further reduced to a lowly 255 a year later. In 1973, it was completely eliminated.

One of the most popular Vettes ever built, the 1963 fastback Sting Ray design is considered a classic today. This particular example is powered by a 327-ci small-block powerplant. The front-end treatment was a dramatic change from that of the previous Corvette generations.

Two 427 engines were available for the 1967 Corvette, with horsepower ratings of 430 and 435, respectively. The model featured the lower body-length exhaust pipes. A convertible model is shown here.

The 427 was called the L36 in 1967, and with the unique tri-carb set-up, the engine was capable of 390 horsepower. The L71 427 included aluminum cylinder heads, and the horsepower increased to 435.

The 1970 Vette differed little from that of the 1969 model. One of the biggest changes was the ice-cube-tray grille design. The standard engine for this model was a 300-horse 350-ci engine.

In 1970, it would have appeared to the outsider that the horsepower race was continuing with the aforementioned 454 engine replacing the 427 family. Such was not the case, though, as only the 390-horsepower LS-5 version was available. The 454-powered Vettes had a sizable opponent, and it also wore the Chevy bowtie. The LT-1 was only 20 horses below the 454, and it was a much more streetable machine. For that and other reasons, just 4,473 LS-5 Vettes were built in 1970. However, the 454 hung around in reduced power versions until 1974. During this period, there was also a reported LS-7 454 powerplant, but the best sources indicated that the engine was never installed in any factory Vettes. Corvette experts surmise that some dealership installations could have occurred.

In 1971, a 425-horse version of the 454, the LS-6, was available. Even though the compression ratio had been appreciably reduced to 9:1, the powerplant was an excellent power-producer because of its large displacement, domed pistons, and 800-cfm Holley carb. The LS-6 proved to be a much better street engine than the early 427 powerplants. It would, however, be available for only this model year, and only 188 were built.

There are still those that will argue the Corvette was not a muscle car during this era. But judging by the powerful small- and big-block powerplants that were available, it's hard not to make the association.

Camaro

Camaro buyers faced a difficult choice in the car's early years: Do I buy Trans Am race-derived Z28, the Super Sport (SS), or Rally Sport (RS)? Many buyers opted for the SS model, which provided the big horsepower capabilities. The SS was available with the Camaro in its initial 1967 model year. If performance was the name of the game, this was the option to pick. For the really big horsepower numbers, however, buyers had to wait a bit during the model year.

When the SS package was first introduced, it came only with the L48 350-ci engine, producing 295 horsepower. But that would all change midyear with the introduction of a pair of 396-ci big blocks: the L35 punching 325 horses and the L78 with 50 more than that. The L35 was fitted to 4,003 Camaros that year and the L78 to 1,138. Maybe the latter wasn't surprising, since the buyer had to plunk down an extra $500 for the additional horsepower.

The L48 350 mill provided plenty of power for the 12,476 buyers that bought the 295-horse version. Although it was not available with the SS option, mention should be made of the L30 327 powerplant, which was available in both 1967 and 1968 and produced 275 horses. The SS Camaros also came with a dynamite suspension system. Big-block SS Camaros also came with heavy-duty engine mounts, rear axle, and clutch.

The SS emblems seemed to be everywhere on the body, sitting in the middle of the blacked-out grille, gas filler cap, and front quarters. When the 396 was ordered, the front-quarter SS badge was replaced with a special 396 Turbo Jet emblem located directly under a Camaro nametag. Throw in the custom hood, blacked-out rear panel, and SS striping, and this was one killer machine. The popularity of the muscular SS continued in 1968, and although the body style remained basically unchanged, there were some subtle changes made. First, instead of the SS emblem embedded in the vertical bumblebee stripes, the number "350" or "396" engine displacement numbers were used.

There was also the so-called "Big Engine" hood, which featured a pair of twin metal inserts featuring four simulated carburetion stacks.

The first Camaro made its appearance in the 1967 model year. With big horsepower and great looks, it was an instant winner. The SS got most of the attention, but there was also another version called the Rally Sport, or RS. The front-end looks of this first Camaro were stunning, as illustrated by this RS.

This '68 Camaro has just about the best of everything. First, it's the top-of-the-line SS model, as identified by the SS on the front quarter. Then, there are those magic 396 engine-displacement numbers, an engine that was available at several different power levels.

Also for 1968, Chevy offered a third 396 powerplant for the Camaro SS: the L35. The L35 was rated at 250 horsepower, halfway between the 325- and 375-horse models. In addition, for the ultimate performance enthusiast, there was the L89, the special 396 mill equipped with aluminum heads, larger valves, and a custom Holley carb. Introduced late in the model year, only 272 were built. Four four-speeds and a pair of automatic transmissions were offered for use with these engines.

Nineteen sixty-nine was the final year of Camaro's first generation, and this year saw the production of the GM pony car billow to 243,085. Camaro's third year looked a lot like its earlier cousins, but there were some refinements with a lightly altered sheet metal sporting sharper bends and curves.

It was again a year of performance with the three optional 396 engines offered for the SS. The standard powerplant was the L48 300-horsepower 350-ci engine, which became a popular choice. The super-rare and super-powerful L89 engine was still available in 1969, but only 311 customers checked off the option. That's not surprising since that engine option cost an additional $710.95, which was about one-fourth the cost of the basic Camaro model.

The 1969 SS option was identified by RPO Z27 and cost an additional $295.95. It included front disc brakes, heavy-duty suspension, the custom hood backed by insulation, wide-oval tires, black and bright accents, detailed engine compartment, and the expected SS badges. A limited number of SS COPO models were built this model year with either factory- or dealer-installed 427 powerplants.

Big changes were instituted in the 1970 model year, but it took awhile to get production started before the new body style was introduced, therefore causing it to be called the 1970 1/2 Camaro. For many, the wait was worth it, while others yearned for the first-generation styling.

The design changes for this first of the new era were significant. The full body-wide grille was gone, replaced with the centered rectangular design, and the headlights were now located outside its confines. The same powerplants of 1969 were again available for 1970. The L48 350 engine was also a popular option because it offered good performance combined with street manners (a *Road & Track* road test showed a capability of 86 miles per hour and 16.6 seconds in the quarter).

A number of the Chevy intermediate and big models in 1970 got the big-block 454. Chevrolet even considered putting that engine in the Camaro, but it didn't happen, although there were a small number of dealer installations. The L48 300-horsepower 350 was a part of the SS option, which also included special accents, power brakes, hood sound insulation, blacked-out grille, and SS emblems on the rear deck, grille, and front quarters.

The '71 Camaro was pretty much an external duplication of the previous year. The downturn in performance was evident as 30 horses (10 percent of the previous year's 300-horse value) were clipped off the L65 powerplant's horsepower

This Hugger Orange and White '69 SS Camaro really lit the racing fires, looking like it was ready to take to the track. The design was highlighted by the wide pair of body-length stripes and the twin louver set on the aft hood.

Several different small-block 350 engines were fitted to the 1969 Camaros, and this 300-horsepower version is one of them. It carried the company name of Turbo-Fire. This particular engine powered a 1969 RS.

rating. A 396 (its actual displacement was 402-ci) could be ordered as the LS-3, but only 1,533 Camaro buyers selected that powerplant option. The SS, costing an extra $313.90 in 1971, included the expected features, but the SS identifying emblems were only on the front quarters and steering wheel.

Monte Carlo

Luxury and elegance were two of the big goals of Chevy engineers when they introduced the brand-new Monte Carlo in 1970. Those goals were certainly achieved, but the Monte Carlo also ended up with one other significant characteristic in certain models. When some big engines were dropped under the these particular Monte Carlo bonnets, the model became a muscle car of sorts, but its performance was far from that of its Chevy brothers because of its extra weight.

The Monte Carlo was introduced quite late in the muscle-car era, and therefore, it didn't have that muscle image for long. The model was immediately

In an amazing occurrence, two of the first three Camaros were given the huge honor of being the pace car for the Indy 500. This is the 1969 version, and the lettering on the door leaves no doubt of its selection. A number of replicas were built (this being one of them) and were powered by a 350 engine.

It wasn't a well-known fact, but a small number of 427-powered Camaros were built. Some of these were factory-built versions called COPOs; others were built by performance dealerships such as Yenko (shown here), Burger, and others. Yenko was the most prolific, with its distinctive body trim and detailing. These models are certainly valuable and exciting.

provided with the 454 engine, so there was no long build-up in power. It got the biggest there was in the Chevy camp right off the bat. That 454 power, the LS5 360-horsepower version being the standard offering in this application, was definitely needed since the Monte Carlo weighed in the neighborhood of 3,500 pounds. It certainly was no match for the other performance cars of the day. Car-magazine tests of the day showed it only had a 16-second capability in the quarter mile. However, if you wanted to plunk down the extra bucks, it was possible to order the 390- and 425-horse versions of the 454.

Besides special suspension equipment, the SS454 package also included the Turbo Hydra-matic transmission and power disc brakes. A black and silver lower trim stripe carried the SS454 designation. Fewer SS454s were sold in 1971, making Chevy wonder if it had made a big mistake with the introduction of the model The LS-5 was the

standard engine for the '71 SS454, with a horsepower rating of 365 horsepower, although the 425-horse LS6 could be ordered as an option. Non-SS Monte Carlos were available with the 245-horsepower 350 and 300-horsepower 402 engines. For the 1971 model, it was as though Chevy was trying to hide the fact that big horses were resting under the longest hood in the Chevy inventory. There was no SS454 identification anywhere on the front of the top-line model to announce its big-block pedigree. Even the emblems that were on the car were practically invisible.

In 1972, the performance-oriented Monte Carlo was stone dead. In fact, anything to do with performance or a racy image was actually mocked in the Monte Carlo national advertising campaign. A greatly degraded 454 powerplant could still be ordered, but it was only putting out 270 net horses. The last year for the 454 was 1975, but by then its horsepower rating had dropped off by half.

The Monte Carlo appeared late in the muscle car era and had several faces. With its stylish stance and impressive front end, it gave the impression of being a luxury car, but with the addition of the powerful 454 engine, there was also a muscle connotation to this machine.

When the 396 was no longer big enough, Chevy introduced the even larger 454. There were two versions of the engine, the LS-5 (shown here) and the awesome LS-6, with 360 and 425 horsepower, respectively.

Chapter 3

Oldsmobile

L ike the other GM divisions, Oldsmobile certainly didn't want to get shut out of the muscle car game, and came forth with its first muscle model: the 442. Several versions of the 442 soon followed, and each soon earned its own fame.

The 442

Everywhere, three-digit numbers flaunted the cubic inches of the giant powerplants they carried (including SS396, 421HO, 440 Six-Pack, and so on). The numbers "442" in Olds lingo meant something entirely different than engine displacement, or even torque. It came down to a specific meaning for each number. The first "4" stood for the four-barrel

Was the 1970 Hurst/Olds an out-of-sight, macho looker of an Olds muscle car? You better believe that it was, decked out in basic white with gold trim on the fender lines and on the center of the hood. Check out those brutish twin hood scoops, which scream big-time performance.

Model year 1964 was the first year for the 442, but it was an option package for the Cutlass, not really a separate model. The numerals "4-4-2" denoted a four-barrel carb, four-on-the-floor transmission, and dual exhausts. In the years to follow, not all 442s would carry all those attributes, but the popular designation would still be used.

carb, the second "4" identified the four-speed fully synchronized transmission with floor-mounted shifter. Finally, there's that last elusive "2." It quite simply stood for the stock dual-exhaust arrangement.

The initial 1964 442 had only 330 cubic inches under the hood, but before the 442 performance era ended, the cubic inches would numerically top the 442 name by 13 cubic inches.

National advertisements proclaimed the 310 horses and 355 pounds-feet from the so-called Jetfire Rocket V-8. This engine featured an impressive

20-horse increase over previous engines of the same displacement, and that extra power really showed itself in performance. Reportedly, the 0–60 time was in the mid-7-second range. Oldsmobile ads touted the excellent handling of its new 442, and the bragging was justified. Heavy-duty springs up front were rated at 410 pounds per inch, while the impressive rating out back was 160 pounds per inch.

Surprisingly, the first 442, like the first Pontiac GTO, was not a separate model. Rather, the 442 was an option for the F-85 Cutlass line. It was called the B-09 option, or Police Pursuit Apprehender, and cost an additional $289.14. With the superb publicity the initial 442 acquired, it was not surprising that Olds engineers would kick up the ponies a bit more for the following 1965 model year. All the 1964 goodies were once again included, but the 330-ci powerplant was replaced with a 345-horsepower 400-ci/screamer. Both the bore and stroke were appreciably increased for the new powerplant, to a 4-inch bore and a 3.98-inch stroke. Compression ratio remained extremely high, at 10.25:1. The new engine was topped with a 700-cfm Quadrajet carburetor, along with a special radiator, 70-amp battery, and dual low-restriction exhausts.

In 1966, the optional L69 powerplant with three two-barrel (300-cfm each) carbs was similar to the famous GTO Tri-Power. A number of these powerplants were retrofitted by dealers and owners. The standard 442 powerplant was again the 400-ci engine, only this year the rating was increased to 350 horsepower, nudged upward by its new 10.5:1 compression ratio.

Only slight changes were made to the body styling with blacked-out tail panel and grille. The 442 emblems were quite noticeable, located on the right rear deck, rear quarters, and grille.

The 442 for 1967 was starting to gain its own distinctive look with a unique grille accented with an embedded 442 emblem. The characteristic fender scoops were gone for this year, but the model now also sported new sport striping on the doors and fenders. The aggressive look was set off with new red-line tires. The tri-carb set-up of the previous year was gone for 1967, but the 350-horse, four-barrel 400 engine with 440 pounds-feet of torque was still available. Also, powertrain upgrades allowed the awesome engine to operate at a much higher efficiency level. A special Turbo Hydra-matic transmission, a stronger 12-bolt rear end (available with 3.42

and 3.91:1 ratios) and F70x14-inch wide-oval tires made the '67 442 a street performer of the first order.

Buyers loved the automatic transmission, and it outsold the four-speed model for the first time. The 442s were also starting to turn heads on the national drag strips, and one even set a National Hot Rod Association (NHRA) B/Pure Stock national record.

For 1968, the news was big in the 442 camp—and for two big reasons. First, the 442 became a separate model on its own, no longer an F-85 option. It even had its own new body style with a 3-inch-shorter wheelbase at 112 inches. The December 1967 *Motor Trend* magazine report described the model as a "Stirring car, full of built-ins and potential for performance enthusiasts." The 400 engine was back again in redesigned form, with a larger bore (4.125 inches) and a considerably smaller stroke (3.385 inches). Horsepower was quoted at 350 horses with a four-speed transmission and 325 with the automatic.

For the 1969 model year, the 442's body lines remained relatively unchanged, but there was a considerably different look to the front end. The grille was halved by body-colored sheet metal upon which was scribed the expected 442 identification. The 442 numerals were also boldly blocked out on the front quarters.

The 442 body design was slightly altered for 1970 and appeared to project more of a refined look. The changes were greatly appreciated by the buying public. The rear bumper carried four slotted vertical taillights, located directly over the stylish dual exhaust extensions. Olds also offered the optional rear-deck-mounted W-35 spoiler.

Additional refinements were made to the front end, including a new vertical pattern in the twin grille. Next came a pair of macho hood scoops on the new W-25 hood, and the neat thing about the scoops was that they were functional. A pair of

Several car magazines voted the 1968 442 as the top performance car of the year, and it was well deserved. The package included a 325-horsepower engine under the hood, heavy-duty suspension, front and rear stabilizers, and wide-oval red-line tires.

This red air cleaner denoted the standard powerplant for the '68 442, a super street and strip performer kicking out 325 horsepower from its 400 ci. With a 10.5:1 compression ratio, four-barrel carb, and dual exhausts, this powerplant was one of the top muscle performers of its time.

The '69 442 was styled for the track. The front end featured a pair of blacked-out openings and a slotted front bumper. The sheet metal was sculpted on the sides, with a macho kickup on the rear quarters. Rakish five-spoke wheels were a final touch to this performance fantasy.

racing-style hood pins added to the performance look. It's easy to understand why many 442 enthusiasts will tell you it didn't get much better than the 1970 442!

The top engine displacement for 1970 was the W34 455 engine with a 4.125-inch bore and a 4.250-inch stroke. Its horsepower was rated an impressive 365, produced at 5,000 rpm. Also, its unbelievable rating of 500 pounds-feet of torque spoke for itself.

Yet there were even more options available to handle the horsepower of this heavy hauler. The M40 Turbo Hydra-matic with the W-26 Hurst dual-gate shifter was a potent combination for the strip or street. The FE3 sport suspension was also state-of-the-art.

Olds ads of the time period understandably put this model on a pedestal. They stated, "Beneath that air scooped, fiberglass hood rumbles as large a V-8 as ever has been bolted into a special performance, production automobile . . . The special hood? It's part of the W-25 package you can order. Do so-while you're still young enough to enjoy it!"

But things started changing with the 1971 model year as the American lust for performance seemed to be fading. Maybe the

For 1969, the GS was offered with a pair of punchy mills: A 400-ci engine producing 340 horsepower at 5,000 rpm and the 350-ci engine shown here, which was capable of 280 horses. Even though the 350 had fewer cubes, it was still capable of impressive performance.

country just lost the mood for hot cars in the environment of the upheaval of the Vietnam War. Apparently, Olds started to go along with that trend of non-performance thinking as the tire-scorching capabilities of the 442 started its downward spiral in 1971. However, Olds wasn't alone when it started yielding to the trend. It was happening everywhere. In previous years, 442 production had accounted for as much as 5 to 6 percent of the total Olds production. In 1971, the 7,589 442s produced accounted for only a miniscule 1.3 percent of the Olds total. Despite these changes, the '71 442, didn't look that much different from its year-earlier muscular brother. That rakish twin-scoop hood, complete with the hood pins, was still in place, and there was a new mesh grille design, which was the only significant external change.

On a whole, major changes were taking place across the industry in the powerplant department. The culprit was low-octane unleaded fuel—something that high-compression engines certainly didn't care for one bit! Also, government-mandated pollution controls were putting a clamp on performance. In order to utilize the wimpy gas, it was necessary for Olds—along with all the other GM divisions—to drop the compression ratio figure by two full digits. That's a bunch, and it's amazing that the horsepower didn't drop more than it did. The power loss in the 455 powerplant was minimal: 25 horses to a still-impressive 340 figure. It was the final year that horsepower was quoted in gross numbers.

For 1972, "performance" seemed a dirty word. The new trend evolving in Olds advertisements was obvious when engine performance wasn't even mentioned until you were almost done reading the ad. "442" this model year meant "A special 442 Sport Handling Package" that could be ordered on four different Cutlass models. The term "package"

in those ads indicated bad news for the 442 as a separate model. After four years as a distinct model during the true muscle era, the 442 was reduced to option status again.

It was not expensive to have your '72 Cutlass garbed as a 442: $71.62 for the Cutlass and $150.61 for the Cutlass Supreme. Both included the Hurst three-speed shifter. The package also included body and rear-deck striping, louvers, and the expected trio of famous number identification. Suspension pieces (carried under the FE Rallye Suspension Package) were heavy-duty springs and shocks, front and rear stabilizer bars, heavy-duty rear lower control arms, and 14x7-inch tires.

New government regulations, high insurance rates for big-engined cars, and the turn toward lower-cost cars had automotive designers looking in different directions. The '72 442 was really starting to feel the pressure. The standard '72 442 powerplant (the L-75) was rated at 270 horsepower. Remember again, those were net horses, so the reduction in performance wasn't as bad as the reduction in numbers would suggest. The equivalent gross-horsepower number was probably approaching 300 horses.

Even in this era of performance downgrading, the 455 engine was still offered. In fact, that engine would be available through the 1976 model year.

Olds "W" Cars

The best way to describe the "W" was "Wild"! That was certainly the case with the number of W versions that spelled performance in a big way for certain 442s and other Olds models.

In the early twenty-first century, such W-modified machines are the most coveted and most valuable of the Olds performance line. Initially, there was no W on the external sheet metal, but Olds quickly realized that 21st letter

Externally, the fact that a particular '69 442 carried the W-30 option was not loudly announced. The W-30 designation was in the body-length striping directly under the 442 numbers on the lower front quarters. Its extra performance certainly deserved more significant attention.

The W-30 option was available with the 455 engine for 1970. The W componentry on this awesome powerplant provided an extra 5 horsepower over the standard 455 mill, possibly much more. The engine was also significant because it had a torque capability of the magic 500 pounds-feet figure.

The muscle era was going away, but the W-30 was still offered for the 1972 model year. The performance decreased with a drop in compression ratio that year, but the W equipment made it about as good as it could get.

identification should be announced for all to see, and the W appeared on later versions. With the initial Olds W machines, it was necessary to lift the hood to firmly ascertain the performance breed. In all, there were three Olds W variants. The most popular was the W-30, along with the W-31 and W-32 versions.

W-30

The W-30 was the most abundant and most recognizable of these Olds performance options. It was offered from the mid-1960s through the early 1970s, only on Olds models, and the package's equipment really set the W models apart from standard Olds performance machines.

The 1966 442 was the first recipient of the W hardware. Interestingly enough, the initial W-30 was added to an existing powerplant that really didn't need it. The powerful L69 442 engine was already hooked with a tri-carb set-up and sure didn't look like it needed any additional ponies. That didn't stop some Olds performance types who added the package to the already potent mill.

The W-30 addition consisted of a unique dual-snorkel air cleaner with a trio of twin-nut depressions. The 5-inch-diameter air cleaner openings hooked to a pair of hoses that traversed forward, outward, and then dropped to lower-bumper openings. Dark, elongated scoops were quite evident in the bumper and subtly indicated what was under the hood. The name of the system was appropriately known as the "Force Air" induction system. But there was more W-30 stuff for 1966. When the

The final year for the W-31 was 1970. Hood scoops replaced the characteristic induction tubes of previous years. Horsepower was advertised at 325, the same as for the standard 442 powerplant, even though the W-31 mill sported an aluminum intake manifold.

W-30 option was ordered with the 400-ci engine, the 440 was fitted with stouter valve springs and a hotter cam, which optimized the powerplant for the W-30 induction system.

Olds benefited in national drag racing when a W-30 L69 won the National NHRA C Stock titles—pretty heavy stuff for the first time out! It's hard to believe that Olds didn't flaunt the W-30 on the car's exterior, but it just didn't happen. So, only the really tuned performance nuts knew about it. That, however, would change in the years to come.

One would have thought that the increasing exposure to the W-30s would have caused the Olds big wigs to vigorously announce its presence, but that wasn't the case in 1967. For 1967, the W-30's second year, the L69 tri-carb engine was gone, so the air cleaner was now mounted on a Rochester four-barrel and it carried a more conventional round air cleaner with a removable top.

Also, a dealer-installed option presented some full-race modifications. The Force Air Induction system was still in place, but there were some changes in the system. A significant modification was required to route the left side tubing. The battery had to be removed to make room, and it was relocated to the trunk. To further enhance the performance of W-30 cars, Olds engineers trimmed a little weight off in a very innovative way: the fiberglass inner fenders were bright red in color. Other subtle changes in the W-30's second year made this machine a real performer on the strip, capable of sub-14-second quarters. A new capacitive discharge ignition system supplied a hotter spark, and a hotter cam with a longer 308-degree duration provid-

ed a fatter charge of fuel and air. The restyled and rakish A-Body design went right along with the power image of the W-30 option for 1968. Also, for the first time, you could even read about the W-30 in the company literature and discover what that magic designation actually meant.

Interestingly enough, there was a note to potential buyers about the rough idle characteristics of the W-30 powerplant and that it might not be ideal for all buyers. Despite that, 1,911 performance-oriented buyers selected the W-30 option. You can bet that every one of those buyers wishes they still had that car today!

For 1968, the induction ducts were moved from the grille to underneath the bumper, and the air cleaner configuration was changed to a twin-snorkel version of the standard 442 air cleaner. Despite the changes, the W-30's power rating was unchanged: a sizzling 360 horsepower. In all, the W-30 componentry added 35 horsepower to the standard 442 powerplant.

The W-30 option included more than just a fancy induction system. Tolerances were extremely tight on W-30 engines, and these engines were mated to limited-slip rear ends that carried ratios up to 4.66:1.

For 1969, the W-30 option was available only on the 442. The 400 powerplant was souped to the hilt with dual air ducts, dual-intake air cleaner, big intake and exhaust valves, and a high-overlap cam. Even with all the upgrades, the horsepower was still listed by the factory at 360. This was the first year that Dr. Olds, a devious-looking character, was used in W-30 advertising.

Next page: Looking down the side of this 1968 Hurst/Olds, a number of the unique features are visible. Note the black striping that runs two-thirds the length of the body, terminating at the front bumper. Also, under-bumper scoops were used to duct cool air into the twin-snorkel air cleaner.

For 1970, the W-30 got the 455 engine. The W-30 components were awarded 5 extra horsepower (370 at 5,200 rpm), a very conservative addition. The trademark induction tubes were replaced by the twin-scoop W-25 fiberglass induction hood. The brand-new 455 featured hydraulic lifters, five main bearings, and dual exhausts that helped it earn a monumental torque rating of 500 pounds-feet at only 3600 rpm. The impressive performance numbers compensated somewhat for the '70 W-30's weight of almost 3,700 pounds.

The '70 W-30 was the ultimate of the W mods in the minds of many collectors. Unfortunately, it was but a final fleeting moment because a serious downturn in performance commenced the following year, as a two-point drop in compression ratio lowered the horsepower rating of the mighty W-30 powerplant by 70 horses to 300.

W-31

For 1968, Olds first offered the W-31 option with the Cutlass and F-85, which souped up small-block powerplants with the same parts and pieces that made the W-30 as great as it was. Interestingly enough, the W-31 option was not available on the 442, which of course carried the Olds performance image. With a twin-snorkel air cleaner, 2-inch-intake heads, and a four-barrel Rochester carb, the W-30's engine produced an impressive 320 horsepower.

The first W-31 engine was called the Ram Rod 350, which was identified with a fender-mounted decal depicting the end view of two pistons, rods, and a crank with the words "Ram Rod 350."

For 1969, the changes were minimal and production was up slightly to 931 units. It was also possible to acquire a W-31 convertible, but few buyers made that choice. A W-31 decal on the front quarters was the only identification. The engine carried a four-barrel Quadrajet carburetor. Its horsepower was increased by 5, to 325.

The W-31's final year was 1970, but that certainly hadn't been the plan of Olds brass. Nevertheless, the 1970 W-31 was the best of the three years the model was in production. New features included chrome medallions and a redesigned fiberglass hood sporting Ram-Air scoops that fed cool air directly into the top of the air cleaner.

W-32

The W story still had one more twist and turn. The W-32 model, which lasted for only two years (1969 and 1970), is often forgotten when the W cars are mentioned. The model was a mid-1969 introduction and was strictly a 442 option, and even then was available only with the 400 engine and Turbo Hydra-Matic 400 automatic transmission.

For the 1969 W-32, the only identification was the W-32 decals located directly above the front quarter marker lights. The W-32 400-ci engine was rated at 350 horses and was fitted with a 286-degree duration, 0.472-inch lift, 58-degree overlap cam, and the Force Air system with the under-bumper scoops. Other unique aspects of this gutsy powerplant included separated center exhaust ports and individually branched exhaust manifolds. The only external identification was a W-32 decal affixed directly above each front-quarter marker light.

In 1970, the W-32 was not available with the 442; instead, it was offered only on the Cutlass Supreme. During that year, the W-32 option included a 455-ci engine mated to an M-40 automatic. For some reason the W-32 decals were deleted, making it somewhat of a lost W machine. Nevertheless, its performance certainly wasn't lost on the select few who ordered the option.

Hurst/Olds

Any mention of the magical name "Hurst," and all kinds of visions come into focus—performance, style, class, and Linda Vaughn! Fortunately for the Olds line, the red and blue block "H" with the oval-encircled "Hurst" featured on a series of specially prepared Hurst/Olds models boasted big-time performance and out-of-sight appearance innovations. The name also carried a solid connection with fans of the muscle car. The Hurst/Olds models appeared six times, but only two times during the muscle years, in 1968 and 1969.

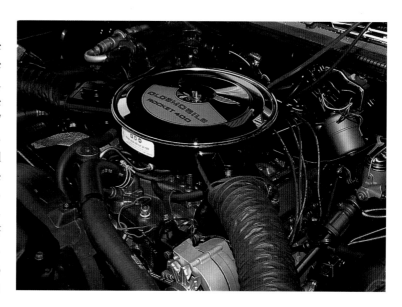

We're talking about a killer powerplant with the '68 Hurst/Olds mill, a 455-ci performer that was capable of punching out an impressive 390 horses and 500 pounds-feet of torque. The powerplant was fitted with hydraulic lifters, 10.25:1 compression ratio, and a high-performance crank and camshaft.

The initial 1968 Hurst model (H/O for short) was just the ticket for the Olds image, and through the years the model has become one of the most desirable of all the vintage muscle models. The biggest of many attractions on the Hurst model was what rested under its bawdy black and silver hood: 455 cubic inches of W-30-style big block pumped out 390 gross horsepower at only 5000 rpm and 500 pounds-feet of torque at 3600 rpm. The engine carried the W-30 Force Air Induction system, with snorkel tubing and under-grille scoops, a high-lift cam, and special carburetor jetting.

With a rear sway bar and heavy-duty suspension components, the 1968 Hurst/Olds also had superb handling. New front disc brakes, equipped with a proportioning valve, added greatly to stopping efficiency. Slap on the Goodyear G70x14s and stand back! The performance was breathtaking. With the 3.91:1 rear end ratio, quarter-mile capabilities were in the high-13-second bracket.

If buyers liked the '68 Hurst/Olds for its radical performance looks, then the '69 Hurst most likely completely blew them away. Where the first H/O's sinister gray and black paint was somewhat drab, the '69 Hurst was a ray of sunshine in gold and bright white. With the white as the base coat, a wide gold band swept across the lower body, along with pointed gold stripes on the upper front and rear fenders, twin stripes up the rear deck, and a single stripe on the hood. This vehicle was a knockout!

The awe-inspiring W-30 455 mill was still in place, but for some reason, Olds now announced its performance at a 10-horse-lower value of 380 horses. The torque was still listed at the same 500 pounds-feet. The March 1969 edition of Car and Driver magazine documented 14.1-second, 100-mph performance in the quarter mile.

73

Chapter 4

Pontiac

Among the GM brands, Pontiac probably shares the top performance image with Chevy. That image was forged by the Grand Prix models and burnished by the GTO, The Judge, and the Firebird/Trans Am models that evolved in the late 1960s and early 1970s.

The GTO

The 1964–1966 GTOs constituted the first generation. They have become muscle classics of the first order and will always hold their high place when the first muscle cars are recalled. It could be said that the GTO came to being on a technicality. In the early 1960s, the Pontiac division operated under an edict that restricted it to

For 1969, the name of the GTO was fitted with an Endura bumper that would assume its original shape after an impact. In 1970, the taillights were installed in the rear bumper. A decal on the rear deck identified the GTO.

75

A LeMans option in 1964, the GTO would soon be a model on its own, and what a model it would be!

fitting standard engines of 330 cubic inches or under. At some point, somebody figured out that the restriction applied only to standard engines, and not to optional engines. One of the first products of this loophole was the GTO, a combination of the new-for-1964 A-body chassis and tuned 389 big-block engines.

Two quick-revving 389-ci powerplants were available in the GTO. They would remain in place, basically unchanged for the GTO's first three

years. One version carried a standard four-barrel carburetor, while the big-publicity version carried a row of three two-barrel carbs, the famous Tri-Power. The Tri-Power's three Rochester 2GC carbs provided a total of 780 cfm and an additional 23 horsepower at 4900 rpm.

Pontiac also upgraded the suspension system of the GTO to include a four-link upper and lower rear control arm set-up, augmented with heavy-duty coil springs. The front end was fitted with a

beefy 15/16-inch stabilizer bar. It should be noted that this first GTO was actually not a model on its own, but an option of the LeMans model. Even so, its long, flowing body lines combined with a twin-opening blacked-out grille to set the standard for the classic muscle looks of the early GTOs.

Years later, the 1965 GTO was voted the most popular GTO of any of the 11 versions produced from 1964 to 1974. The four-barrel 396 engine was now rated at 335 horses, the increased performance coming from a higher-lift 288-degree

The top-gun powerplant for the '64 GTO was this Tri-Power 389, which had a vacuum set-up for bringing the two outer carbs on line. Unfortunately, the system didn't work that well. For that reason, many owners replaced the factory set-up with a mechanical linkage. When perking to perfection, the Tri-Power engine was capable of 348 horses. A four-barrel version of the powerplant produced 325 horses.

The 1966 GTO sported a revised front end that gave the third-year GTO a completely new look. The grille recesses were deeper, and the parking lights were mounted on the grille-opening mesh material. The grille recesses were also outlined with chrome trim. That infamous GTO name was buried in the left grille recess.

cam. Minor changes were also made in the head and intake-port deck heights, and a Carter AFB four-barrel carb was now standard. The same three Rochester two-barrels were again in place for the Tri-Power version, but the 1965 version was rated at 360 horsepower, 12 more than in 1964. The major appearance change in the model was the stacking of the headlights.

For 1966, louvered taillights were the major appearance change. The popular twin-opening grille remained unchanged.

Bigger changes were made for 1967. The body was restyled, and a 400 replaced the 396 in the engine compartment. Compared to the old 396, the new 400 engine featured a larger bore and redesigned cylinder heads. In standard form

78

Sadly, the triple carbs were gone after 1966, but the 400 HO powerplant shown here was a worthy replacement. With a special cam and valvetrain, the powerplant was rated at 360 horses.

for the GTO, it was rated at 335 horsepower. Yet, for some reason the 400 just didn't seem to have the charisma of the 389, which had generated a cult following.

The new 400 engine was also available as the 400 HO, which was rated at 360 horses. Drawing on some older classic Pontiac technology, the headers were quite similar to the earlier Super Duty versions of the early 1960s. A hotter cam and open-element air cleaner also added punch to an

engine that would soon have performance enthusiasts exclaiming about its virtues.

But if you really wanted to light your fire, you had to try the other 400 engine, the 400 Ram-Air. Even though the 400 Ram-Air wasn't fitted with the three two-barrels of the Tri-Power 396, it was given a functional hood scoop, a hotter cam, and 4.33:1 rear end. Despite all these additions, the 400 Ram-Air was rated at the same 360 horsepower as the HO.

For 1968, the GTO featured a completely restyled chassis with bumpers made of Endura plastic. In its application to the new front-end design, the flexible space-age material was able to absorb low-speed front-end impacts and bounce back to its original shape. In a bold update, the headlights were hidden in blackout grille openings with lids opening when the lights were activated. The centered single hood scoop of the previous year was replaced by dual scoops.

Horsepower was plentiful from three monster powerplants. The standard 400-ci engine was up-rated to 350 horses at 5,000 rpm with an awesome 444 pounds-feet of torque. The HO and Ram-Air 400s returned with a few refinements in 1968, but the same power ratings as it had in 1967. A series of automatic and manual transmissions, along with numerous rear end ratios, could be assembled for just about every customer's performance fantasy.

Late in the '68 model year, Pontiac kicked up the power again, replacing the Ram-Air 400 engine with the new Ram-Air II powerplant, which sported a hotter cam, new round-port heads, a Rochester Quadrajet carburetor, a hydraulic cam, and forged aluminum pistons. It was rated at 366 horsepower. Although the Ram-Air induction system was a factory option, it was not installed at the factory. Rather, it arrived in the trunk for dealer installation. All these changes for 1968 won the GTO *Car and Driver's* award for the Best All-Around Car and Best Sports Design.

Next, for the final GTO of the decade, Pontiac made appreciable changes to the GTO's exterior, the majority of them to the rear end. The vertical portion of the rear deck, including the taillights, was completely encased with chrome stripping.

For the 1969 model year, the so-called Ram-Air III engine replaced the Ram-Air II. Updates to the III included D-Port heads, all-weather ram-air

scoops that could be closed off in case of rain, and a Rochester Quadrajet carburetor. Making 366 horsepower and identified with Ram-Air decals, the Ram-Air III was another rocket, slightly faster than the Ram-Air II of the previous model year, and capable of a magazine-tested best quarter-mile clocking of 14.10 seconds.

Ask any GTO performance enthusiast and you'll quickly learn that the Ram-Air IV, introducedin 1969, was the ultimate of the 400 engines. With many upgrades—including aluminum heads, a hotter cam, stiffer pushrods, all-weather ram-air

system, and four-bolt mains, the Ram-Air IV was beautifully balanced and a terror for any confrontation. The fact that it was rated at only 4 horsepower over the Ram-Air III was a joke!

Many said that the '69 Ram-Air IV was the fastest of all the muscle GTO versions. Capable of 6.6-second performance to 60 mph, the IV could cut the quarter mile in less than 14 seconds.

For 1970, the big GTO news was the initial use of a 455-ci powerplant. The big block would be around through the 1973 model, but with greatly reduced power. In 1970, however, the 455 HO was rated at a very respectable 360 horsepower. It could ordered with either a three- or four-speed manual or the Turbo Hydra-Matic transmissions. Also available were the standard, Ram-Air III, and Ram-Air IV 400 engines. Strangely, it was also possible to order the Ram-Air equipment with the 455 engine, but there were no internal engine changes made when that engine choice was made. Surprisingly, the new 455 wasn't making the horsepower expected from its greater displacement. Rated at "only" 360 horsepower, the 455 was less powerful than the Ram-Air 400-ci powerplants. Appearance-wise, the 1970

The 1965 GTO was definitely built to attract the youth culture. It was quite different from the 1964 and 1966 versions.

GTO's more aggressive and deeply recessed grille and dramatic sculptured side sheet metal transformed the car's look. Although horsepower ratings were down throughout the industry for 1971, the GTO for that year was still muscle-bound, even after meeting strenuous new emission requirements for the year and modifications for the car to run on lower-octane regular gasoline.

General Motors decided that the best way to cope with the new low-power petrol was to lower compression ratios. Needless to say, it required a significant lowering. For the 455 engines, compression was reduced to a lowly 8.4:1. Emissions were further reduced for 1971 on the 455 HO engine by sealing the carburetor's mixture-adjustment screw and adding a new sensor arrangement that shut the automatic choke off more quickly during start-up. With all these changes in the name of economy and reduced emissions, performance fans dreaded to hear what effect the changes would have on quarter mile clockings. For sure, the good old days with high 13-second runs would definitely be a thing of the past. What the changes actually meant in terms of horsepower was a drop to 300 (from 350) for the 400 engine and to 335 for the 455 HO.

Styling-wise, the '71 GTO took on a completely new look in the front end. It was actually more racy looking than the '70 model, even though the 1971 engines couldn't back up their looks like the 1970 engines could.

In the years to follow, GTO performance grew steadily less impressive. Yet, during its day, the GTO was right up there with the best, in both performance and appearance.

An interesting footnote must be added to the GTO story, one that didn't take place in the factory: During the 1960s, a number of dealerships specialized in performance upgrades of existing GM models. Royal Pontiac, of Royal Oak, Michigan, was the prime Pontiac dealership for such activities, and its products became known as "Royal Bobcats." Small name medallions on the front quarters identified the GTOs that were so endowed.

Royal Pontiac offered a number of performance packages during the 1960s GTO performance years. Most notable of these was the substitution of a 421-ci engine for the stock 389 engine. These replacement engines were created at over 400 horsepower. Other modifications included the tweaking of the stock engines for greater performance. In 1968, Royal offered a 428 HO engine swap for only $650. A March 1964 *Car and Driver* test of a GTO Bobcat with the 421 engine showed amazing performance of 13.1 seconds at 115 mph in the quarter mile.

Compared to the total GTO production, the numbers of the Royal Bobcats was small, making them a great investment in the twenty-first century. Basically, an already great muscle machine was made to be even better.

The Judge

Returning to the pure factory GTOs, there has to be mention made of the Judge, which was basically a gussied-up GTO. Even so, it was a GTO model that stood on its own. You owned the Judge, not a GTO!

Pontiac transformed the standard GTO into the Judge halfway into the 1969 model year, with the intention of making it a single-year model. Its popularity prompted Pontiac to keep it in the line-up through the 1971 model year. The reasoning behind the Judge design was that the new GTO variation might attract the younger set with its visual appeal, specifically garish colors and unique detailing. "The Judge" emblems on each front fender, on the right side of the 60-inch-wide rear spoiler, and on the dash set this special car apart

Color styling for the first 1969 Judge was considerably different from the final two versions. A distinctive multi-colored stripe stretched from the front of the fender and followed the line of the windows, terminating on the high rear quarter. It really spruced up the conservative GTO exterior.

The biggest difference between 1969 and 1970 Judges is in the side-stripe design. Where 1969 models had a single stripe stretching two-thirds the length of the body, 1970 Judges had two eyebrow stripes. A 60-inch-wide spoiler across the rear deck really set off this machine.

Eye-catching "The Judge" emblems on the front fenders and on the rear deck spoiler announced that this was not a regular GTO. When the model was discussed, it was called "The Judge," and not the "GTO Judge."

This 1970 Judge was fitted with the same 366-horsepower 400-ci 366 horsepower Ram-Air III engine that was available on the '69 GTO.

from the more pedestrian GTOs. A distinctive stripe that swept along the top of the front fenders, across the doors, and finished in a flared kick-up further distinguished the Judge.

In addition to visuals, performance was an equally important part of the formula for the Judge, so the initial 1969 model carried the Ram-Air III powerplant. The even-more-potent Ram-Air IV was also an option. Officially released to the public in December 1968, the comparison to the standard GTO was quickly made by the buying public. The lineage was definitely there, but it looked like a distant cousin, and it was a rowdy cousin at that!

The first 2,000 of the '69 Judges were painted an eye-catching Carousel Red, but later the Judge was available in any GTO color. The Judge cost just over $300 more than the equivalent GTO.

An even-more distinctive look came on board with 1970's Judge. A pair of twin eyebrow stripes, located on the front and rear fenders, anointed each side of the car. "The Judge" decals appeared on the lower front fenders and on the right side of the rear deck.

For the final 1971 model, the Judge remained basically unchanged from the previous version. The same teardrop striping was still in place, and the fact that the vehicle was carrying the LS5 455 HO was announced on each edge of the rear spoiler. An interesting footnote on 1971's Judge must be included: 15 models were produced in Cameo White with black striping and rear wings. The cars were built under RPO 604, and their extreme rarity makes them highly desirable to collectors.

Changes were minimal for the 1968 Firebird, but when you've got a winner design, why mess with success? This side view shows a '68 Firebird convertible and the sculpting running down the side of the machine.

The Firebird and Trans Am

The Firebird was the first Pontiac trip into the sports-car market, but it was created under a significant design handicap. The division was forced to design its first Firebird, and a number of succeeding models, with Camaro sheet metal. But even with this constraint, the early Birds had a distinctive look of their own.

The first Firebird, introduced in 1967, featured horizontally mounted headlights resting within the recesses of a distinctive blacked-out grille. The rear of the Bird was also unique, never to be mistaken for the Camaro. In that first Firebird, the top-performance small block was a 285-horsepower 326-ci powerplant. It was a part of the HO option, which cost an additional $280 and which included appearance and performance items.

Several experts have stated that the HO engine might have approached the 300-horse figure. Looking at the engine components—Carter four-barrel carb, dual exhausts, and a 10.5:1 compression ratio—might tend to verify that opinion. The HO body was also distinctively signified with a body-length horizontal stripe and an embedded "HO" identification.

But if you wanted the top-dog performance engine of the 1967 Birds, the Firebird 400 was the ticket, with an offered choice of two different 325-horse engine versions. The Ram-Air version, which added an additional $263 to the option sheet, featured functional hood scoops. Hood scoops were also included with the base 400, but they were

Following page
The first Trans Am was introduced in 1969 and sometimes carried both the Firebird and Trans Am names on the front quarters. The L-67 was the standard engine for the Trans Am, but the car could be ordered with the more-powerful Ram-Air powerplants.

The '69 Ram-Air III L-74 engine (shown here) was available with the first Trans Am and was advertised with a 335-horsepower rating. The Ram-Air IV offered an additional 10 ponies and is considered the ultimate by collectors.

During the early 1970s, the Firebird line presented a number of models that flaunted both styling and performance. The integration of air dams into the lower front end is evident in this photograph.

For the 1971 Firebird, engine displacement was up to 455, and the 455HO LS-5 made good use of the displacement, with 355 horsepower at 5,200 rpm. The engine featured an 8.4:1 compression ratio and a functional cool-air induction system.

Although performance was down for the 1972 Firebird, the looks were still there. With those twin blacked-out grilles and those hood-hugging scoops, it just didn't get any better!

Whether a '73 Firebird was carrying the SD-455 powerplant or not, this was a great-looking machine. Note the molded lower front spoiler and the flairs directly in front of the rear wheelwell opening.

non-functional. Both engines were rated at 410 pounds-feet of torque.

Nineteen sixty-eight would have to be called a year of subtle refinement for the Firebird; if you didn't look carefully, it was really difficult to detect the external differences between the two model years. The major difference was body side marker lights (in the form of the Pontiac medallion) that appeared on the rear quarters. The 350 HO powerplant provided a pleasurable punch with an impressive 320 horsepower. The numbers were great for a small block, and close to the high-performance

standard for the day of 1 horsepower for each cubic inch.

A pair of 400-ci engines proved to be the hot tickets for the 1968 Firebird line. The standard engine was called the Firebird 400, but to really light your fire, there was the Ram-Air version. Again, there was minimal difference horsepower-wise, only 5 to be exact, with the Ram-Air version rated at 335 horses at 5,000 rpm. A second version of the Ram-Air engine was introduced near the end of the model year, the Ram-Air II. The Ram-Air II might have been called an upgrade, but it was effectively

a new powerplant. It was definitely full-race, with four-bolt main bearings, special manifolds, and forged pistons.

Nineteen sixty-nine was also a year of transition. Most importantly, 1969 was the model year that the Firebird line established itself as a distinct model, no longer just a sheet metal copycat of the Camaro. This distinction was accomplished through a complete restyling, both inside and out. Next came the introduction of the Ram-Air III and Ram-Air IV powerplants.

Also important was the introduction of the high-level Trans Am model, which would prove to be the star of the Firebird line in the years to come.

The Trans Am was available in only one color combination, a smashing white base color complemented with a pair of body-centered wide blue racing stripes. The base Firebird 400 carried the potent 330-horse W-66 engine (an output that was only 5 horses more than that of the 350 HO engine). The 400 engine was capable of considerably more torque at 430 pounds-feet versus 380 for the 350 HO.

The next step up was the 335-horse Ram-Air 400 engine, which could be ordered under option code 348. Carrying the L-74 engine designation, the Ram-Air 400 carried a special de-clutching fan. A point of confusion existed with this engine, as it

Nineteen seventy-three saw the introduction of the powerful 455 Super Duty engine, at a time when the muscle was dropping off in just about every other model. The horsepower was advertised at 290, a figure that was grossly underrated. The NHRA listed the powerplant at 375 horses, a more reasonable figure in the minds of most.

basically was the famous Ram-Air III, along with also being called the 400 HO. Whatever it was called, it required buyers to cough up $435 for its purchase. Also, as in the GTO, the Ram-Air IV L-67 engine was available. Ram-Air IVs were rated at 345 horsepower, but the engine's torque rating was the same as for the Ram-Air III.

In 1970, the new Formula 400 made its appearance, and it was available with both the base 400 (330 horsepower) and the Ram-Air III (now advertised at 335 horsepower). It was also available with the Ram-Air IV, although that engine had to be special ordered.

Trans Ams for 1970 featured a single stripe on the center body, but the color scheme was flipped and featured a blue body with a white stripe.

In 1971, there was a continuation of Firebird performance, even though it was supposed to be the downturn year because of the new smog retirements. On the contrary, 1971 was the year big-block 455 engines were introduced. The two trends just didn't seem to mesh. It was interesting

to note that the 455 displacement figure for the Firebird exceeded the maximum 454 number for the Camaro line.

The Trans Am for 1971 looked very much like the previous year's model, but the standard powerplant was the 455 HO engine, with an identifying decal on the shaker hood scoop.

The LS5 455 was the top powerplant for the model year, with the net horsepower figures rated at 300. When the net figure quoted for 1971 is converted to the gross figure previously quoted, however, the figure approaches 330. Quarter-mile performance was still in the 14-second bracket.

In an amazing change of direction, the 1973 and 1974 model years saw Pontiac introduce its out-of-step LS-2 SD-455 Super Duty engine. Internally, this was a full-race mill, which the division had advertised as having 290 net horsepower and 395 pounds-feet of torque. Right in the middle of the gas crunch, this powerplant seemed completely out of touch with the atmosphere of the time period.